BEN FROG'S BIRTHDAY PARTY

Tamika Royster

Ben Frog's Birthday Party

by Tamika Royster

Illustrations by
Ella Loren Bulatao

Edited by
Charles H. Styer

Inspirational Quote:

Whatever it is that you desire in life, go forward regardless of the challenge. It only appears hard to accomplish, because it's a part of your destiny. No good thing takes place without an effort.

Ben Frog:

"It's another boring birthday for me. I really don't see the big fuss about them. Every year I do the same things. First I wake up. Second I fix me a bowl of Frosted Fly Flakes. Last I get dressed in my swimsuit, and off to the pond I go. My friends usually hang out with me every day, but I haven't heard from Harry, Toby, or Marcie. I guess they're all busy today; so I will just go ahead to the pond without them."

Meanwhile, Ben Frog has no idea that his friends, Marcie Rabbit, Toby Bear, and Harry Rabbit, were preparing a surprise party. It was all planned out with cake, balloons, food, and fun.

Toby Bear (Singing):
> "Blowing up balloons, takes a lot puffs.
> Red, Yellow, Green, and Blue, have we got enough?
> Huff and blow, up they go.
> Tie them in a knot, ooh…that's hot!
> Birthdays are lots of fun.
> Plenty of balloons for everyone."

Marcie Rabbit:

"I'm sure by now Toby has finished with all of the other decorations? We are almost done! I know Ben is going to be so excited when he sees all that we have done. I must hurry and get this cake in the oven. I can't wait to see Ben's face when he sees all that we have done for his special day!"

Just as Toby Bear was finishing up the balloons, Marcie Rabbit comes up behind him.

Marcie Rabbit:

"Toby are you finished with all of the other decorations?"

Toby Bear:

"Yes, we're all set! I'm about to take the balloons and hang them up all around the pond. I even have a few to go up in the trees. Ben will be so excited."

Marcie Rabbit:

"Great job, Toby! I've got the cake in the oven, and it's just about time for it to come out. (Singing). I baked a cake as fast as the baker's man, and rolled it up and threw it in a pan. (Laughing). As soon as it's ready I will bring it down to the pond. We must hurry! It's about time for Ben to come to the pond. I know by now he is wondering where we are."

Harry Rabbit was waiting for the others down at the pond grilling carrots, fish, fly dogs and some other goodies for Ben Frog's birthday party. There were a few other animals around swimming and playing waiting for the party to begin.

Harry Rabbit:

"Old Mr. Harry had a grill EIEI…O, and on that grill he has some links EIEI…O… A fly link here and a fly link there, everywhere, everywhere, everywhere a fly link. Old Mr. Harry had a grill EI…EI…O…....!"

Marcie Rabbit:

"Harry and Toby! Hurry, hurry! I just saw Ben Frog coming through the path. He was in his swimsuit, so I know he's headed to the pond."

Toby Bear:

"Okay. Everyone in your places!"

Harry Rabbit:

"The food is all done, and the table is set and ready."

Everyone gets really quiet. They all listen while Ben Frog sings loudly as he heads toward the pond.

Ben Frog:
> "A head for nodding, shaking, and thinking; Eyes for seeing, closing, and blinking.
> Ears for hearing, nice things or boring; a nose for smelling, blowing, and snoring.
> A mouth for speaking, eating, and kissing; Teeth for chewing, but my front teeth are missing.
> Arms for waving, hugging, and squeezing; Hands for clapping, helping, and, sneezing.
> Elbows and knees for bending and stretching; Legs for kicking, running, and fetching.

Right at the bottom my two little feet; for dancing and tapping a musical beat."

Ben Frog comes around the corner out of the trees. Everyone screams, "Happy Birthday! Surprise!"

Ben Frog:

"Wow!!! Is all this for me? Thanks so much! I've never had a party."

Ben Frog runs over to the table where the cake and all the other goodies sit. He sits down and joins the others as they eat and laugh, enjoying the party.

The End

Test Yourself

1. When Ben Frog did not hear from his friends what did he think?

    a) they went to the mall

    b) they went to the beach

    c) they forgot his birthday

    d) they all were mad at him

2. Which order does Ben Frog put his swimsuit on?

    a) first

    b) second

    c) third

    d) none of the above

3. What was Toby Bear's job for the party?

    a) ordering pizza

    b) to bake a cake

    c) to grill the food

    d) blow up balloons

4. What did Harry Rabbit cook on the grill?

    a) carrots

    b) fish

    c) fly dogs

    d) all of the above

5. Where did Marcie, Toby, and Harry have Ben's birthday party?

       a) at Ben's house

       b) the bowling alley

       c) by the pond

       d) in forest

I would like to dedicate this book to my three amazing children Wajaya, Javian, and Christnah. You can do anything that you desire to do in this life regardless of how big or small. Do not limit yourself or allow others to determine how far you can go. God has giving us all the power of a sound mind with gifts and talents to be discovered, so use them wisely. You all are blessed and highly favored.
Love You,
Mom

www.ingramcontent.com/pod-product-compliance
Lightning Source LLC
LaVergne TN
LVHW072116070426
835510LV00002B/83